# Start with Art

# Sculptures

Isabel Thomas

730

Raintree

**www.raintreepublishers.co.uk**
Visit our website to find out
more information about
Raintree books.

**To order:**
☎ Phone 0845 6044371
🖹 Fax +44 (0) 1865 312263
🖳 Email myorders@raintreepublishers.co.uk

Customers from outside the UK please telephone +44 1865 312262

Raintree is an imprint of Capstone Global Library Limited,
a company incorporated in England and Wales having its
registered office at 7 Pilgrim Street, London, EC4V 6LB –
Registered company number: 6695582

Edited by Dan Nunn, Rebecca Rissman, and Catherine Veitch
Designed by Richard Parker
Picture research by Mica Brancic and Hannah Taylor
Originated by Capstone Global Library
Printed and bound in China by South China Printing
   Company Ltd

ISBN 978 1 406 22407 8
15 14 13 12 11
10 9 8 7 6 5 4 3 2 1

**British Library Cataloguing in Publication Data**
Thomas, Isabel
Sculptures. -- (Start with art)
730-dc22
A full catalogue record for this book is available from
the British Library.

**Acknowledgements**
We would like to thank the following for permission to
reproduce photographs: Alamy Images pp. 10 (© Seasonalpik),
13 (© Janine Wiedel Photolibrary), 17 (© South West Images
Scotland); Bridgeman Art Library p. 11 (Ancient Art and
Architecture Collection Ltd.); © Capstone Publishers pp. 4, 12,
20, 21, 22, 23 materials, 23 natural materials, 23 tools (Karon
Dubke); Corbis pp. 6 (Kay Nietfeld/epa), 8 (Art on File/©
Anish Kapoor. All Rights Reserved, DACS 2011. Cloud Gate,
2004, Anish Kapoor, Stainless steel, 33 ft x 66 ft x 42 ft.
Millennium Park, Chicago. Courtesy of the artist, City of
Chicago and Gladstone Gallery), 16 (Werner Forman), 18
(Ted Soqui); 19 Krijn de Koning; Photolibrary pp. 7 (Britain on
View/Roger Coulam), 9 (Age fotostock/Jose Antonio Jimenez),
14 (View Pictures/Grant Smith); Shutterstock pp. 5 (© Jorge
Sanchez Torrado), 23 three-dimensional (© Abraham
Badenhorst), 23 kiln (© Anistidesign), 23 subject
(© Nastenok); 15 (© Sokari Douglas Camp. All rights
reserved, DACS 2011).

Front cover photograph of the Angel of the North sculpture by
Antony Gormley reproduced with permission of Photolibrary
(Britain on View/Alan Novelli). Back cover photographs of
clay and natural materials reproduced with permission of ©
Capstone Publishers (Karon Dubke).

Every effort has been made to contact copyright holders
of material reproduced in this book. Any omissions will
be rectified in subsequent printings if notice is given to
the publisher.

All the Internet addresses (URLs) given in this book were valid
at the time of going to press. However, due to the dynamic
nature of the Internet, some addresses may have changed, or
sites may have changed or ceased to exist since publication.
While the author and publisher regret any inconvenience this
may cause readers, no responsibility for any such changes can
be accepted by either the author or the publisher.

# Contents

Some words are shown in bold, **like this**. You can find
out what they mean by looking in the glossary.

# What is a sculpture?

A sculpture is a **three-dimensional** piece of art.

You can walk around a sculpture and look at it from different sides.

People have made sculptures for thousands of years.

Some old sculptures are very big.

# Where can I see sculptures?

Museums collect sculptures from different times and places.

Visit a museum to get ideas for making your own sculpture.

You can find sculptures everywhere.

This sculpture is next to a busy main road. Millions of people see it every year.

# What do people use to make sculptures?

Many artists make sculptures out of metal, stone, and wood.

These hard **materials** last for a long time, even if the sculpture is outside.

Sculptures can be made out of almost anything.

This sculpture of a puppy is made out of flowers!

# What else can I use to make sculptures?

Try making sculptures out of things that you find.

This artist used **natural materials**, such as leaves and twigs, and other **materials**.

Clay sculptures are made all around the world.

This clay sculpture of a lion is 4,000 years old.

# How do people make clay sculptures?

Clay is a soft material.

You can make shapes and patterns using **tools** or your hands.

kiln

Clay goes hard when it dries.

Artists can bake clay sculptures in a **kiln** to make them tougher.

# Why do people make sculptures?

Sculptures help artists to show other people their ideas.

This sculpture shows the artist's ideas about water.

Sculptures can tell us about life in other places.

This sculpture shows the bright colours and clothes of Africa.

# What can sculptures show?

Sculptures can show us what a **subject** really looks like.

They help us to remember important people like kings and queens.

Sculptures do not have to look real.

This sculpture uses shapes to show how kings and queens are different from other people.

# How can sculptures make you feel?

Some sculptures are funny and surprising.

They make you think new of things.

Sculptures can make you feel curious, excited, happy, or sad.

How does this sculpture make you feel?

# Start to make sculptures!

Use **natural materials** to make art like the sculpture on page 10.

1. Look at minibeasts in books or real life. What shapes, colours, and patterns can you see?

2. Collect different materials from a garden or park. Look for twigs, leaves, seeds, feathers, petals, and stones.

3. Find a thick piece of cardboard to use as a base.

4. Use your materials to make minibeast sculptures. Cut shapes to make wings, legs, stripes, and spots.

5. When you are happy with your sculpture, join the parts together with glue.

6. Display your natural art in a garden or park!

# Glossary

**kiln**  very hot oven used to bake clay models to make them hard

**materials**  things you use to make art, such as paper and clay

**natural materials**  things that you find in nature, such as stones, twigs, and leaves

**subject**  person, place, or object shown in a piece of art

**three-dimensional**  not flat

**tools**  things you use to make art, such as pencils and crayons

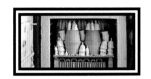

# Find out more

**Book**

*Action Art: Sculpting,* Isabel Thomas (Raintree, 2005)

**Website**

On this website you can explore models made by modern artists:
www.moma.org/interactives/destination/

# Index